AF269853

GREATEST OF ALL TIME PLAYERS

G.O.A.T. HOCKEY DEFENDERS

Josh Anderson

Lerner Publications ◆ Minneapolis

Lerner Publications Company
An imprint of Lerner Publishing Group, Inc.
241 First Avenue North
Minneapolis, MN 55401 USA

For reading levels and more information, look up this title at www.lernerbooks.com.

Main body text set in Aptifer Sans LT Pro.
Typeface provided by Linotype AG.

Library of Congress Cataloging-in-Publication Data

Names: Anderson, Josh, author.
Title: G.O.A.T. hockey defenders / Josh Anderson.
Other titles: Greatest of all time hockey defenders
Description: Minneapolis, MN : Lerner Publications, 2024. | Series: Lerner sports. Greatest of all time players | Includes bibliographical references and index. | Audience: Ages 7–11 | Audience: Grades 2–3 | Summary: "Hockey's best defenders block shots, disrupt passes, and lay big hits on opposing skaters. How do you rank the greatest of all-time? Explore their careers, examine their stats, and then make your own G.O.A.T. list"— Provided by publisher.
Identifiers: LCCN 2023019241 (print) | LCCN 2023019242 (ebook) | ISBN 9798765610251 (library binding) | ISBN 9798765623626 (paperback) | ISBN 9798765614945 (epub)
Subjects: LCSH: Hockey players—Canada—Biography—Juvenile literature. | Hockey players—United States—Biography—Juvenile literature. | Hockey defenders—Biography—Juvenile literature. | BISAC: JUVENILE NONFICTION / Biography & Autobiography / Sports & Recreation
Classification: LCC GV848.5.A1 A643 2024 (print) | LCC GV848.5.A1 (ebook) | DDC 796.962092/2—dc23/eng/20230420

LC record available at https://lccn.loc.gov/2023019241
LC ebook record available at https://lccn.loc.gov/2023019242

Manufactured in the United States of America
1 – CG – 12/15/23

TABLE OF CONTENTS

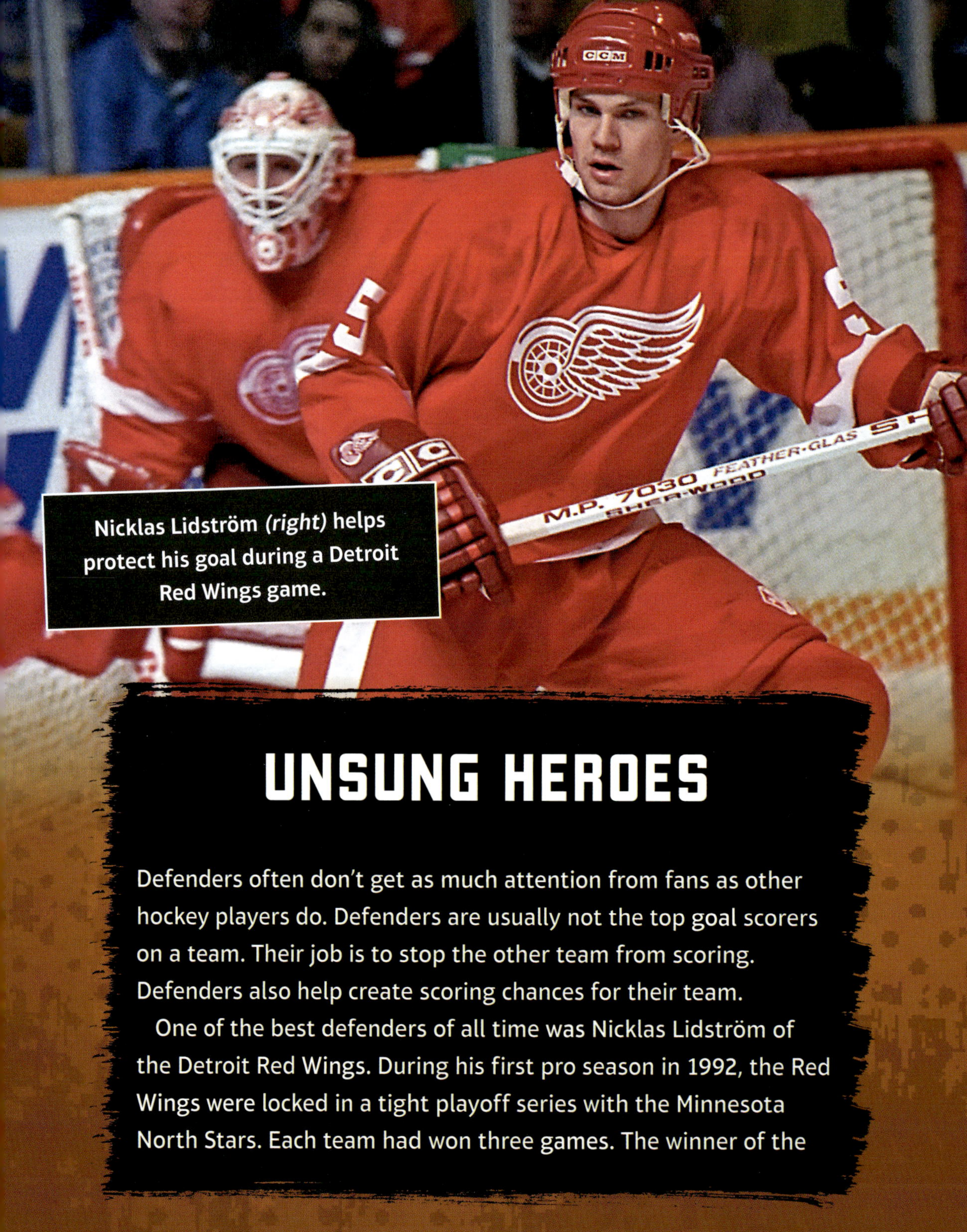

UNSUNG HEROES

Defenders often don't get as much attention from fans as other hockey players do. Defenders are usually not the top goal scorers on a team. Their job is to stop the other team from scoring. Defenders also help create scoring chances for their team.

One of the best defenders of all time was Nicklas Lidström of the Detroit Red Wings. During his first pro season in 1992, the Red Wings were locked in a tight playoff series with the Minnesota North Stars. Each team had won three games. The winner of the

FACTS AT A GLANCE

» **RAY BOURQUE** HAS MORE GOALS THAN ANY OTHER DEFENDER IN NATIONAL HOCKEY LEAGUE (NHL) HISTORY.

» THE ALL-TIME LEADER IN PLUS/MINUS IS DEFENDER **LARRY ROBINSON**.

» **GERALDINE HEANEY** WAS THE THIRD WOMAN TO JOIN THE HOCKEY HALL OF FAME.

» **CHRIS PRONGER** OF THE ST. LOUIS BLUES WON THE HART MEMORIAL TROPHY AS THE NHL'S MOST VALUABLE PLAYER (MVP) IN 2000. NO DEFENDER HAS WON THE AWARD SINCE.

seventh game would move on to the next round of the playoffs.

With Detroit up 1–0 in the second period, Lidström took the puck from Minnesota. With three North Stars surrounding him, he passed the puck across the ice to a teammate. Seconds later, Detroit scored. The Red Wings went on to win the game 5–2. Lidström's play had led to a huge goal for his team. But fans

might not have noticed because he didn't score a goal or get an assist.

Fans and teams track players' stats to help judge how players perform. One way to see a defender's performance is through the plus/minus stat. It shows how often a player is on

Colorado Avalanche defender Cale Makar takes a shot.

the ice when their team scores or is scored against. The higher
the number, the more often the team scores when that player
is on the ice. Lidström ranks eighth all-time in plus/minus. But
was he the greatest of all time (G.O.A.T.)? Or does that honor
belong to another superstar defender? Let's find out!

CALE MAKAR

Cale Makar is one of the best young players in the NHL. The Colorado Avalanche chose Makar with the fourth overall pick in the 2017 NHL Draft. He played two seasons at the University of Massachusetts before joining the Avalanche in 2019.

Makar's first game with the Avalanche was during the 2019 Stanley Cup Playoffs. He scored a goal in the first period to help Colorado beat the Calgary Flames 6–2. Makar played 57 games for the Avalanche in the 2019–2020 season. He won the Calder Memorial Trophy as the league's top rookie.

Makar helped the Avalanche win the Stanley Cup in 2022. That season, he won the Norris Trophy as the year's best defender and the Conn Smythe Trophy as the MVP of the playoffs. Makar finished fifth in the NHL with a 48 plus/minus in 2021–2022. He ranked 16th that season with 58 assists. Makar also plays for Team Canada. He led the team to a gold medal at the 2018 World Junior Championships.

CALE MAKAR STATS

Goals	65
Assists	181
Plus/Minus	93
NHL All-Star Games	2

Stats are current through the 2022–2023 NHL season.

CHRIS PRONGER

Chris Pronger won the Hart Memorial Trophy for the 1999–2000 season. He was the first defender to win the award in nearly 30 years. No defender has won it since.

Pronger began his career when the Hartford Whalers picked him second overall in the 1993 NHL Draft. He spent nine of his NHL seasons with the St. Louis Blues. Pronger was always one of the biggest and strongest players on the ice. He used his size and strength to help control the game.

Pronger appeared in the Stanley Cup Finals with three different teams. He won the title with the Anaheim Ducks in 2007. He also helped Team Canada win gold medals at the 2002 and 2010 Winter Olympics. In 2015, Pronger joined the Hockey Hall of Fame. Two years later, the NHL picked him as one of its top 100 players of all time.

CHRIS PRONGER STATS

Goals	157
Assists	541
Plus/Minus	183
NHL All-Star Games	5

GERALDINE HEANEY

Geraldine Heaney was one of the best hockey defenders of all time. She led Team Canada to victory in seven straight Women's World Championships between 1990 and 2001. Heaney also led Canada to a silver medal at the 1998 Olympics and a gold medal in 2002.

Heaney excelled on defense, and she was also great at scoring goals. In 125 games for Team Canada, Heaney had 27 goals and 66 assists. She holds the Canadian record for goals, assists, and points for a defender in World Championship play.

As a pro, Heaney played for the Toronto Aeros. She led the team to six championships. Heaney was the Ontario Women's Hockey Federation's top defender three times. After she retired in 2004, the Aeros retired Heaney's jersey number. No Aeros player will wear 91 again. In 2013, Heaney became the third woman to join the Hockey Hall of Fame.

GERALDINE HEANEY STATS

Team Canada Goals	27
Team Canada Assists	66
Team Canada Plus/Minus	93
Team Canada Games Played	125

DENIS POTVIN

The New York Islanders selected Denis Potvin first overall in the 1973 NHL Draft. He played his entire 15-year career for the team and led them to four straight Stanley Cups from 1980 to 1983. Only the Montréal Canadiens have won more titles in a row.

Potvin won the Norris Trophy three times. He was often a key part of New York's scoring efforts. His 310 career goals rank fifth among all defenders in NHL history. When he retired after the 1987–1988 season, he ranked first all-time among defenders with 742 assists. He is the first player in NHL history to record at least 100 assists during the NHL playoffs.

Potvin became part of the Hockey Hall of Fame in 1991. In 2017, the NHL picked him as one of its top 100 players of all time.

DENIS POTVIN STATS

Goals	310
Assists	742
Plus/Minus	456
NHL All-Star Games	9

LARRY ROBINSON

Larry Robinson played 17 of his 20 seasons for the Montréal Canadiens. During that time, he helped lead the team to six Stanley Cup titles.

A Hall of Famer, Robinson is the NHL's all-time leader in plus/minus with 722. His 120 plus/minus in 1976–1977 is the second-highest in a single season. He won the Norris Trophy twice. He also won the Conn Smythe Trophy in 1978.

Nicknamed Big Bird because he stood 6 feet 4 (1.9 m), Robinson's 750 assists are the ninth-most ever by a defender. He played in the NHL playoffs in each of his 20 seasons in the league. That's tied for the most ever by a player.

In 2017, the NHL chose Robinson as one of its 100 best players of all time. After his playing career, Robinson won two more Stanley Cups as an assistant coach and one as a head coach with the New Jersey Devils, and another as an assistant coach of the St. Louis Blues.

LARRY ROBINSON STATS

Goals	208
Assists	750
Plus/Minus	722
NHL All-Star Games	10

PAUL COFFEY

Paul Coffey played for eight teams over his 21-season NHL career. He spent seven seasons with the Edmonton Oilers and led the team to three Stanley Cup titles. He won one more title during his five years with the Pittsburgh Penguins.

Hall of Famer Coffey was known as a scoring defender. He was good at helping his team score and preventing the other team from scoring. He ranks second all-time among defenders in goals, assists, and points. Coffey's 1,135 career assists rank sixth among all players. He won the Norris Trophy three times.

His 48 goals in 1985–1986 are the most ever for a defender in a single season. And Coffey is the only defender to score at least 40 goals in a season more than once.

When the NHL chose Coffey as one of its top 100 players of all time, part of the reason was his amazing games in the NHL playoffs. Coffey has more goals and points in the NHL playoffs than any other defender in history.

PAUL COFFEY STATS

Goals	396
Assists	1,135
Plus/Minus	298
NHL All-Star Games	14

DOUG HARVEY

Doug Harvey helped the Montréal Canadiens win six Stanley Cup titles during his 14 seasons with the team. He also played for the New York Rangers, Detroit Red Wings, and St. Louis Blues during his 19-year career.

Harvey brought a new style of play to hockey in the 1940s, 1950s, and 1960s. Before then, defenders passed the puck to teammates as soon as they received it. But Harvey preferred to control the puck. Like many modern defenders, Harvey skated up the ice to help set up his team's offense. That's one reason why the NHL chose him as one of its top 100 players of all time.

Harvey won the Norris Trophy seven times, tied with Nicklas Lidström for the second-most of any player. Only Bobby Orr won the award more times. Harvey joined the Hockey Hall of Fame in 1973.

DOUG HARVEY STATS

Goals	88
Assists	452
Plus/Minus	46
NHL All-Star Games	13

NICKLAS LIDSTRÖM

Nicklas Lidström spent his entire 20-year career with the Detroit Red Wings. They never missed the playoffs with Lidström on the team. The Hall of Famer's 20 playoff appearances led to four Stanley Cups for Detroit. In 2002, Lidström became the first European-born player to win the Conn Smythe Trophy.

Lidström won the Norris Trophy seven times. That is tied for second-most all-time. He ranks eighth among all players with a 450 plus/minus. Lidström also ranks sixth in assists and points, and eighth in goals among NHL defenders.

Teammates called Lidström the Perfect Human. They believed he played without making any errors. When the NHL named its top 100 players of all time in 2017, Lidström was included. In 2022, he became Detroit's vice president of hockey operations.

NICKLAS LIDSTRÖM STATS

Goals	264
Assists	878
Plus/Minus	450
NHL All-Star Games	11

RAY BOURQUE

Ray Bourque played most of his pro career with the Boston Bruins. In more than 20 seasons with the Bruins, he failed to win a Stanley Cup. Finally, in his last NHL season in 2000–2001, Bourque won his first Stanley Cup. Playing for the Colorado Avalanche, he became a champion for the first time at 40.

Bourque is the NHL's record holder for goals, assists, and points by a defender. Among all players, he ranks third all-time with a 527 plus/minus and fourth with 1,169 assists. Bourque also took the second-most shots in NHL history. Only Alex Ovechkin has taken more.

Bourque is part of the NHL's 2017 list of the top 100 players of all time. The Hall of Famer won the Norris Trophy five times. His 19 NHL All-Star teams are the second-most of all time.

RAY BOURQUE STATS

Goals	410
Assists	1,169
Plus/Minus	527
NHL All-Star Games	19

BOBBY ORR

Bobby Orr played only 12 seasons in the NHL, but he completely changed the game. In his 10 seasons with the Boston Bruins, he showed off his speed and skill. He could score and defend like no other player in NHL history.

Orr's overtime goal in Game 4 of the 1970 Stanley Cup Finals won the Bruins their first Stanley Cup since 1941. He led the Bruins to another Stanley Cup in 1972. After both title-winning seasons, Orr won the Conn Smythe Trophy.

Orr led the NHL in scoring twice. He's the only defender ever to do so. He holds the record for the most Norris Trophy awards. He won the honor eight seasons in a row from 1967–1968 to 1974–1975. Orr also won the Hart Memorial Trophy three times during his career.

Hall of Famer Orr's plus/minus of 582 ranks second in NHL history. In 2017, the NHL named him one of its top 100 players of all time.

BOBBY ORR STATS

Goals	270
Assists	645
Plus/Minus	582
NHL All-Star Games	7

There have been so many amazing defenders throughout hockey history. Choosing only 10 is a challenge. Here are 10 others who could have made the G.O.A.T. list.

....

No. 11	CHRIS CHELIOS
No. 12	EDDIE SHORE
No. 13	SCOTT STEVENS
No. 14	ROB BLAKE
No. 15	SCOTT NIEDERMAYER
No. 16	MEGAN KELLER
No. 17	ERIK KARLSSON
No. 18	BÖRJE SALMING
No. 19	ZDENO CHÁRA
No. 20	ART ROSS

YOUR G.O.A.T.

It's your turn to make a G.O.A.T. list of hockey defenders. If some of your favorite players aren't defenders, make a list for another position too! You can also make a G.O.A.T. list for movies, books, and other things you like.

Start by doing research. You can check out the Learn More section on page 31. The books and websites listed there will help you learn more about hockey players of the past and present. You can also search online for even more information about great players.

Once you have your list, ask friends or family to create a list too. Compare them and see how they differ. Do your friends have different opinions about the greatest players? Talk it over and decide whose G.O.A.T. list is your favorite.

GLOSSARY

assist: a pass leading to a goal

Conn Smythe Trophy: the NHL's award for MVP of the playoffs

draft: when teams take turns choosing new players

Hall of Famer: a player honored in the Hockey Hall of Fame in Toronto, Canada

Hart Memorial Trophy: the NHL's season MVP award

Norris Trophy: the NHL's award for best defender of the season

plus/minus: a stat that shows how often a player is on the ice when their team scores or is scored against

point: a goal or an assist

rookie: a first-year player

Stanley Cup Finals: the NHL's championship series

stat: an item of information

title: a championship

LEARN MORE

Britannica Kids—Ice Hockey
https://kids.britannica.com/kids/article/Ice-Hockey/353257

Doeden, Matt. *G.O.A.T. Hockey Teams*. Minneapolis: Lerner Publications, 2021.

Fishman, Jon M. *Hockey's G.O.A.T.: Wayne Gretzky, Sidney Crosby, and More*. Minneapolis: Lerner Publications, 2020.

NHL official site
https://www.nhl.com/

Sports Illustrated Kids—Hockey
https://www.sikids.com/hockey

Williamson, Ryan. *NHL Hot Streaks*. Mankato, MN: Child's World, 2019.

INDEX

PHOTO ACKNOWLEDGMENTS

Image credits: Graig Abel/Contributor/Getty Images, p.4; Graig Abel/Contributor/ Getty Images, p.5; Michael Martin/Contributor/Getty Images, p.6; Steve Babineau/ Contributor/Getty Images, p.7; Ethan Miller/Staff/Getty Images, p.8; Bruce Bennett/ Staff/Getty Images, p.9; Dave Sandford/Stringer/Getty Images, p.10; Jamie Squire/ Staff/Getty Images, p.11; B Bennett/Contributor/Getty Images, p.12; Brian Bahr/Staff/ Getty Images, p.13; B Bennett/Contributor/Getty Images, p.14; B Bennett/Contributor/ Getty Images, p.15; B Bennett/Contributor/Getty Images, p.16; Focus On Sport/ Contributor/Getty Images, p.17; Graig Abel/Contributor/Getty Images, p.18; Focus On Sport/Contributor/Getty Images, p.19; B Bennett/Contributor/Getty Images, p.20; Pictorial Parade/Staff/Getty Images, p.21; Bruce Bennett/Staff/Getty Images, p.22; Dave Reginek/Contributor/Getty Images, 23; B Bennett/Contributor/Getty Images, p.24; Brian Bahr/Staff/Getty Images, p.25; B Bennett/Contributor/Getty Images, p.26; Robert Shaver/Bruce Bennett Collection/Contributor/Getty Images, p.27

Cover: Michael Martin/Contributor/Getty Images; Graig Abel/Contributor/Getty Images; Michael Martin / Contributor/Getty Images